AF480203

THIS JOURNAL BELONGS TO:

____

Welcome to Your
2-Minute Bullet Journal!

I'm Neeramitra Reddy - the creator of the Journal you're holding right now.

Despite knowing the INCREDIBLE power of journaling, I lacked **Patience** and **Time**.

The online "Bullet Journaling" templates neither appealed to me nor proved effective.

So, I created my own template - and honed it over 6+ months to this **2-Minute** Version.

This Journal's goal is to help you find your **Priorities**, set **Realistic** To-Do's aligning with your **Long-Term** goals, get **More** done, and grow **Grateful.**

 **A Free Exclusive 5-In-1 Bonus For You**

Scan the QR code on the right to grab your free 5-In-1 Journaling + Productivity Bonus pack.

P.S. ONLY buyers of this journal can access this bonus - a private token of my gratitude :)

Be loyal to this journal - It will infuse your life with **Mental Clarity** and **Fulfilment** ☺

Ready?

Time to find your priorities. The next page will show how.

The **3/25 Technique** to Laser In on Your **Top 3 Priorities**

Without Priority, there's no Productivity

Here's a simple exercise to find your top 3 priorities:

- On the next page, list down 10 of your top goals. Don't overthink — go off the top of your head.
- Think and add 7 more to the list.
- Squeeze out another 8.

Filled all 25 goals?

Good! Now, start slashing them:

- Strike out the 10 least important goals.
- Cut out another 7 of your darlings.
- Murder another 3 goals.
- The last stretch - lop off another 2.

The 3 Goals Left Are Your Top 3 Priorities

Jot them down below in descending order:

Priority 0 (P0): ___________________________

Priority 1 (P1): ___________________________

Priority 2 (P2): ___________________________

For Instructions, refer to the **Previous Page**.

1. ______________________________
2. ______________________________
3. ______________________________
4. ______________________________
5. ______________________________
6. ______________________________
7. ______________________________
8. ______________________________
9. ______________________________
10. ______________________________
11. ______________________________
12. ______________________________
13. ______________________________
14. ______________________________
15. ______________________________
16. ______________________________
17. ______________________________
18. ______________________________
19. ______________________________
20. ______________________________
21. ______________________________
22. ______________________________
23. ______________________________
24. ______________________________
25. ______________________________

Priorities sorted? Let's dive into the journal!

The Journal Overview

Section 1: Your Priorities

You'll repeat the 3 "P0/1/2" priorities from the 3/25 rule every day → To internalize them better.

- Priority 0 (P0) :
- Priority 1 (P1) :
- Priority 2 (P2) :

Section 2: The Day's To-Dos/Tasks

Only 4 total daily *ToDo* items → So, we neither overcommit nor undercommit.

- Priority 0 (P0) related tasks:
    - Item 1
    - Item 2
- Priority 1 (P1) related tasks:
    - Item 3
- Priority 2(P2) related tasks:
    - Item 4

Section 3: Gratitude

Recall 3 things, events, or people to be thankful for.

- I'm grateful for X
- I'm grateful for Y
- I'm grateful for Z

How Best To Use This Journal?

You can bullet journal...

- **Right After Your Morning Routine [BEST]**
  I journal after working out + cold showering + breath-work + meditating.

- **Or Before going to Bed [EXCELLENT]**
  Pop this journal on your bedside table. Reflect on the day's positives & visualize/plan the next day's tasks.

- **Or First Thing After Waking Up [GOOD]**
  Place this journal atop your phone - so you bullet journal instead of scrolling after waking up;)

Bonus Tips and Best Practices:

- Noting the same 3 priorities every single day *will* feel repetitive - that's by design. Trust the process.

- Laser-focus on the 4 Tasks you set. Fight the temptation to add more.

- Be it a Bali beach-house or the corner cafe, take this journal along *everywhere.*

  Can't? Journal on your phone's Notes app - or mentally.

No Excuse to Miss Even a Single Day

FAQs 

In What Order Should I Work on The Tasks?

- Start with your P0 tasks. ONLY once they're done, move on to P1. Finally, pick the P2 tasks.
  - *Completing 1 P0 Task >> Half-Ass*ng all 4.*

Can I Parallelize or Batch Tasks?

- P0s demand DEDICATED focus. Batch-finish your P1 & P2 tasks if they're "shallow."
- Parallelization? Futile
  - *Multitasking = Multidistracting* .

How to Fill the Gratitude Section?

- Recall 3 things you felt thankful for the previous day...
  - Food. Loved ones. A kind act you saw. Or a compliment from a stranger.
  - Don't just recall - RELIVE the memory 
- *Even on bad days, you will find positives*

What About Any Leftover Tasks?

- Move them over to the next day. If new *higher-priority* tasks come up, pick accordingly.

Missed the Exclusive Bonus from Earlier?

Here's your friendly QR Code again.

Don't miss it this time, though - this QR code won't reappear again in this journal.

You're All Equipped. Journal Away!

Any further questions? Email me at manximize@gmail.com

Date:__/__/____

My Priorities

Priority 0 (P0): ___________________________________

Priority 1 (P1) : _________________________________

Priority 2 (P2): __________________________________

The Day's Tasks

P0 Tasks :

☐

☐

P1 Task : ☐

P2 Task : ☐

🪷 Daily Gratitude

★ I'm grateful for _______________________________

★ I'm grateful for _______________________________

★ I'm grateful for _______________________________

Date:__/__/____

My Priorities

Priority 0 (P0): ___________________________________

Priority 1 (P1) : ___________________________________

Priority 2 (P2): ___________________________________

The Day's Tasks

P0 Tasks :

☐

☐

P1 Task : ☐

P2 Task : ☐

🪷 Daily Gratitude

✳ I'm grateful for ___________________________________

✳ I'm grateful for ___________________________________

✳ I'm grateful for ___________________________________

Date:__/__/____

My Priorities

Priority 0 (P0): _______________________________________

Priority 1 (P1) : _______________________________________

Priority 2 (P2): _______________________________________

The Day's Tasks

P0 Tasks :

- _______________________________________ ☐

- _______________________________________ ☐

P1 Task : _______________________________________ ☐

P2 Task : _______________________________________ ☐

Daily Gratitude

★ I'm grateful for _______________________________________

★ I'm grateful for _______________________________________

★ I'm grateful for _______________________________________

Date:__/__/____

My Priorities

Priority 0 (P0):

Priority 1 (P1) :

Priority 2 (P2):

The Day's Tasks

P0 Tasks :

☐

☐

P1 Task :   ☐

P2 Task :   ☐

❁ Daily Gratitude

✦ I'm grateful for

✦ I'm grateful for

✦ I'm grateful for

Date:___/___/_____

My Priorities

Priority 0 (P0): ____

Priority 1 (P1) : ____

Priority 2 (P2): ____

The Day's Tasks

P0 Tasks :

☐

☐

P1 Task : ☐

P2 Task : ☐

🪷 Daily Gratitude

⭐ I'm grateful for ____

⭐ I'm grateful for ____

⭐ I'm grateful for ____

Date:__/__/____

My Priorities

Priority 0 (P0): ____

Priority 1 (P1) : ____

Priority 2 (P2): ____

The Day's Tasks

P0 Tasks :

☐

☐

P1 Task : ☐

P2 Task : ☐

Daily Gratitude

✦ I'm grateful for ____

✦ I'm grateful for ____

✦ I'm grateful for ____

Date:__/__/____

My Priorities

Priority 0 (P0):

Priority 1 (P1) :

Priority 2 (P2):

The Day's Tasks

P0 Tasks :

P1 Task :

P2 Task :

❁ Daily Gratitude

✴ I'm grateful for

✴ I'm grateful for

✴ I'm grateful for

Date:__/__/____

My Priorities

Priority 0 (P0):

Priority 1 (P1) :

Priority 2 (P2):

The Day's Tasks

P0 Tasks :

☐

☐

P1 Task : ☐

P2 Task : ☐

Daily Gratitude

✳ I'm grateful for

✳ I'm grateful for

✳ I'm grateful for

Date:__/__/____

My Priorities

Priority 0 (P0):

Priority 1 (P1) :

Priority 2 (P2):

The Day's Tasks

P0 Tasks :

☐

☐

P1 Task : ☐

P2 Task : ☐

Daily Gratitude

★ I'm grateful for

★ I'm grateful for

★ I'm grateful for

Date:__/__/____

My Priorities

Priority 0 (P0): ________________________________

Priority 1 (P1) : ________________________________

Priority 2 (P2): ________________________________

The Day's Tasks

P0 Tasks :

- ☐
- ☐

P1 Task : ☐

P2 Task : ☐

Daily Gratitude

⭐ I'm grateful for ________________________________

⭐ I'm grateful for ________________________________

⭐ I'm grateful for ________________________________

Date:__/__/____

My Priorities

Priority 0 (P0): ______________________________________

Priority 1 (P1) : ______________________________________

Priority 2 (P2): ______________________________________

The Day's Tasks

P0 Tasks :

- ______________________________________ ☐

- ______________________________________ ☐

P1 Task : ______________________________________ ☐

P2 Task : ______________________________________ ☐

🪷 Daily Gratitude

✫ I'm grateful for ______________________________________

✫ I'm grateful for ______________________________________

✫ I'm grateful for ______________________________________

Date:__/__/____

My Priorities

Priority 0 (P0): ____

Priority 1 (P1) : ____

Priority 2 (P2): ____

The Day's Tasks

P0 Tasks :

☐

☐

P1 Task : ☐

P2 Task : ☐

❁ Daily Gratitude

✦ I'm grateful for ____

✦ I'm grateful for ____

✦ I'm grateful for ____

Date:__/__/____

My Priorities

Priority 0 (P0): ______________________________________

Priority 1 (P1) : ______________________________________

Priority 2 (P2): ______________________________________

The Day's Tasks

P0 Tasks :

- ______________________________________ ☐

- ______________________________________ ☐

P1 Task : ______________________________________ ☐

P2 Task : ______________________________________ ☐

Daily Gratitude

★ I'm grateful for ______________________________________

★ I'm grateful for ______________________________________

★ I'm grateful for ______________________________________

Date:__/__/____

My Priorities

Priority 0 (P0): ____

Priority 1 (P1) : ____

Priority 2 (P2): ____

The Day's Tasks

P0 Tasks :

☐

☐

P1 Task : ☐

P2 Task : ☐

Daily Gratitude

✴ I'm grateful for ____

✴ I'm grateful for ____

✴ I'm grateful for ____

Date:__/__/____

My Priorities

Priority 0 (P0): _______________________________

Priority 1 (P1) : _______________________________

Priority 2 (P2): _______________________________

The Day's Tasks

P0 Tasks :

☐

☐

P1 Task : ☐

P2 Task : ☐

Daily Gratitude

⭐ I'm grateful for _______________________________

⭐ I'm grateful for _______________________________

⭐ I'm grateful for _______________________________

Date:__/__/____

My Priorities

Priority 0 (P0): ____

Priority 1 (P1) : ____

Priority 2 (P2): ____

The Day's Tasks

P0 Tasks :

☐

☐

P1 Task : ☐

P2 Task : ☐

Daily Gratitude

★ I'm grateful for ____

★ I'm grateful for ____

★ I'm grateful for ____

Date:__/__/____

My Priorities

Priority 0 (P0): ____

Priority 1 (P1) : ____

Priority 2 (P2): ____

The Day's Tasks

P0 Tasks :

- ____ ☐

- ____ ☐

P1 Task : ____ ☐

P2 Task : ____ ☐

Daily Gratitude

☆ I'm grateful for ____

☆ I'm grateful for ____

☆ I'm grateful for ____

Date:__/__/____

My Priorities

Priority 0 (P0): _______________________________

Priority 1 (P1) : _______________________________

Priority 2 (P2): _______________________________

The Day's Tasks

P0 Tasks :

☐

☐

P1 Task : ☐

P2 Task : ☐

✿ Daily Gratitude

✳ I'm grateful for _______________________________

✳ I'm grateful for _______________________________

✳ I'm grateful for _______________________________

Date:__/__/____

My Priorities

Priority 0 (P0): ________________________________

Priority 1 (P1) : ________________________________

Priority 2 (P2): ________________________________

The Day's Tasks

P0 Tasks :

- ☐

- ☐

P1 Task : ☐

P2 Task : ☐

🪷 Daily Gratitude

★ I'm grateful for ________________________________

★ I'm grateful for ________________________________

★ I'm grateful for ________________________________

Date:__/__/____

My Priorities

Priority 0 (P0): _______________________________________

Priority 1 (P1) : _______________________________________

Priority 2 (P2): _______________________________________

The Day's Tasks

P0 Tasks :

☐

☐

P1 Task : ☐

P2 Task : ☐

Daily Gratitude

* I'm grateful for _______________________________________

* I'm grateful for _______________________________________

* I'm grateful for _______________________________________

Date:__/__/____

My Priorities

Priority 0 (P0): _______________________________________

Priority 1 (P1) : _______________________________________

Priority 2 (P2): _______________________________________

The Day's Tasks

P0 Tasks :

- ☐
____

- ☐
____

P1 Task : ☐
____

P2 Task : ☐
____

Daily Gratitude

★ I'm grateful for _______________________________________

★ I'm grateful for _______________________________________

★ I'm grateful for _______________________________________

21 Days In

It takes 21 days to build a habit. Consecutive or not, if you've made it this far...

Congratulations on Your New Journaling Habit!

"We first make our habits. Then our habits make us."
– John Dryden

 ## Help Others Build Their Journaling Habit

An **Amazon Rating** and **Review** would mean a lot to me and help others discover this journal.

All it takes is scanning the QR code on the right – and a few seconds of your time.

Thank you, my friend.

Don't let this milestone be an excuse to slack. Instead...

Let it fuel your consistency *further*.

Date:__/__/____

My Priorities

Priority 0 (P0): _______________________________________

Priority 1 (P1) : _______________________________________

Priority 2 (P2): _______________________________________

The Day's Tasks

P0 Tasks :

- ☐

- ☐

P1 Task : ☐

P2 Task : ☐

🪷 Daily Gratitude

✦ I'm grateful for _______________________________________

✦ I'm grateful for _______________________________________

✦ I'm grateful for _______________________________________

Date:__/__/____

My Priorities

Priority 0 (P0): ____________________________

Priority 1 (P1) : ____________________________

Priority 2 (P2): ____________________________

The Day's Tasks

P0 Tasks :

☐

☐

P1 Task : ☐

P2 Task : ☐

🪷 Daily Gratitude

✳ I'm grateful for ____________________________

✳ I'm grateful for ____________________________

✳ I'm grateful for ____________________________

Date:__/__/____

My Priorities

Priority 0 (P0): _________________________________

Priority 1 (P1) : _________________________________

Priority 2 (P2): _________________________________

The Day's Tasks

P0 Tasks :

☐

☐

P1 Task : ☐

P2 Task : ☐

Daily Gratitude

★ I'm grateful for _________________________________

★ I'm grateful for _________________________________

★ I'm grateful for _________________________________

Date:__/__/____

My Priorities

Priority 0 (P0):

Priority 1 (P1) :

Priority 2 (P2):

The Day's Tasks

P0 Tasks :

☐

☐

P1 Task : ☐

P2 Task : ☐

Daily Gratitude

✳ I'm grateful for

✳ I'm grateful for

✳ I'm grateful for

Date:___/___/_____

My Priorities

Priority 0 (P0):

Priority 1 (P1) :

Priority 2 (P2):

The Day's Tasks

P0 Tasks :

- ☐

- ☐

P1 Task : ☐

P2 Task : ☐

Daily Gratitude

★ I'm grateful for

★ I'm grateful for

★ I'm grateful for

Date:__/__/____

My Priorities

Priority 0 (P0):

Priority 1 (P1) :

Priority 2 (P2):

The Day's Tasks

P0 Tasks :

☐

☐

P1 Task : ☐

P2 Task : ☐

Daily Gratitude

⭐ I'm grateful for

⭐ I'm grateful for

⭐ I'm grateful for

Date:__/__/____

My Priorities

Priority 0 (P0): ___________________________

Priority 1 (P1) : ___________________________

Priority 2 (P2): ___________________________

The Day's Tasks

P0 Tasks :

- ☐

- ☐

P1 Task : ☐

P2 Task : ☐

🪷 Daily Gratitude

⭐ I'm grateful for ___________________________

⭐ I'm grateful for ___________________________

⭐ I'm grateful for ___________________________

Date:__/__/____

My Priorities

Priority 0 (P0):

Priority 1 (P1) :

Priority 2 (P2):

The Day's Tasks

P0 Tasks :

☐

☐

P1 Task : ☐

P2 Task : ☐

Daily Gratitude

✶ I'm grateful for

✶ I'm grateful for

✶ I'm grateful for

Date:__ / __ / ____

My Priorities

Priority 0 (P0): ______________________________

Priority 1 (P1) : ______________________________

Priority 2 (P2): ______________________________

The Day's Tasks

P0 Tasks :

☐

☐

P1 Task : ☐

P2 Task : ☐

Daily Gratitude

★ I'm grateful for ______________________________

★ I'm grateful for ______________________________

★ I'm grateful for ______________________________

Date:__/__/____

My Priorities

Priority 0 (P0): ______________________________

Priority 1 (P1) : ______________________________

Priority 2 (P2): ______________________________

The Day's Tasks

P0 Tasks :

☐

☐

P1 Task : ☐

P2 Task : ☐

Daily Gratitude

I'm grateful for ______________________________

I'm grateful for ______________________________

I'm grateful for ______________________________

Date:__/__/____

My Priorities

Priority 0 (P0): ____

Priority 1 (P1) : ____

Priority 2 (P2): ____

The Day's Tasks

P0 Tasks :

☐

☐

P1 Task : ☐

P2 Task : ☐

🪷 Daily Gratitude

★ I'm grateful for ____

★ I'm grateful for ____

★ I'm grateful for ____

Date:__/__/____

My Priorities

Priority 0 (P0): ____

Priority 1 (P1) : ____

Priority 2 (P2): ____

The Day's Tasks

P0 Tasks :

☐

☐

P1 Task : ☐

P2 Task : ☐

Daily Gratitude

✳ I'm grateful for ____

✳ I'm grateful for ____

✳ I'm grateful for ____

Date:__/__/____

My Priorities

Priority 0 (P0): ___________________________

Priority 1 (P1) : ___________________________

Priority 2 (P2): ___________________________

The Day's Tasks

P0 Tasks :

- ☐

- ☐

P1 Task : ☐

P2 Task : ☐

Daily Gratitude

★ I'm grateful for ___________________________

★ I'm grateful for ___________________________

★ I'm grateful for ___________________________

Date:__/__/____

My Priorities

Priority 0 (P0):

Priority 1 (P1) :

Priority 2 (P2):

The Day's Tasks

P0 Tasks :

☐

☐

P1 Task : ☐

P2 Task : ☐

Daily Gratitude

✳ I'm grateful for

✳ I'm grateful for

✳ I'm grateful for

Date:__/__/____

My Priorities

Priority 0 (P0): ____

Priority 1 (P1) : ____

Priority 2 (P2): ____

The Day's Tasks

P0 Tasks :

☐

☐

P1 Task : ☐

P2 Task : ☐

Daily Gratitude

★ I'm grateful for ____

★ I'm grateful for ____

★ I'm grateful for ____

Date:__/__/____

My Priorities

Priority 0 (P0):

Priority 1 (P1) :

Priority 2 (P2):

The Day's Tasks

P0 Tasks :

☐

☐

P1 Task : ☐

P2 Task : ☐

Daily Gratitude

✵ I'm grateful for

✵ I'm grateful for

✵ I'm grateful for

Date:__/__/____

My Priorities

Priority 0 (P0): ____

Priority 1 (P1) : ____

Priority 2 (P2): ____

The Day's Tasks

P0 Tasks :

- ____ ☐

- ____ ☐

P1 Task : ☐

P2 Task : ☐

✿ Daily Gratitude

★ I'm grateful for ____

★ I'm grateful for ____

★ I'm grateful for ____

Date:__/__/____

My Priorities

Priority 0 (P0):

Priority 1 (P1) :

Priority 2 (P2):

The Day's Tasks

P0 Tasks :

☐

☐

P1 Task : ☐

P2 Task : ☐

Daily Gratitude

✦ I'm grateful for

✦ I'm grateful for

✦ I'm grateful for

Date:__/__/____

My Priorities

Priority 0 (P0): ____

Priority 1 (P1) : ____

Priority 2 (P2): ____

The Day's Tasks

P0 Tasks :

- ☐

- ☐

P1 Task : ☐

P2 Task : ☐

Daily Gratitude

★ I'm grateful for ____

★ I'm grateful for ____

★ I'm grateful for ____

Date:__/__/____

My Priorities

Priority 0 (P0):

Priority 1 (P1) :

Priority 2 (P2):

The Day's Tasks

P0 Tasks :

⬜

⬜

P1 Task : ⬜

P2 Task : ⬜

Daily Gratitude

⭐ I'm grateful for

⭐ I'm grateful for

⭐ I'm grateful for

Date:__/__/____

My Priorities

Priority 0 (P0): ____

Priority 1 (P1) : ____

Priority 2 (P2): ____

The Day's Tasks

P0 Tasks :

- ____ ☐

- ____ ☐

P1 Task : ____ ☐

P2 Task : ____ ☐

🪷 Daily Gratitude

⭐ I'm grateful for ____

⭐ I'm grateful for ____

⭐ I'm grateful for ____

Date:__/__/____

My Priorities

Priority 0 (P0): ____

Priority 1 (P1) : ____

Priority 2 (P2): ____

The Day's Tasks

P0 Tasks :

☐

☐

P1 Task : ☐

P2 Task : ☐

Daily Gratitude

✳ I'm grateful for ____

✳ I'm grateful for ____

✳ I'm grateful for ____

Date:__/__/____

My Priorities

Priority 0 (P0): ______________________________

Priority 1 (P1) : ______________________________

Priority 2 (P2): ______________________________

The Day's Tasks

P0 Tasks :

- ______________________________ ☐

- ______________________________ ☐

P1 Task : ______________________________ ☐

P2 Task : ______________________________ ☐

Daily Gratitude

☆ I'm grateful for ______________________________

☆ I'm grateful for ______________________________

☆ I'm grateful for ______________________________

Date:__/__/____

My Priorities

Priority 0 (P0):

Priority 1 (P1) :

Priority 2 (P2):

The Day's Tasks

P0 Tasks :

☐

☐

P1 Task : ☐

P2 Task : ☐

Daily Gratitude

✳ I'm grateful for

✳ I'm grateful for

✳ I'm grateful for

Date:__/__/____

My Priorities

Priority 0 (P0): ________________________________

Priority 1 (P1) : ________________________________

Priority 2 (P2): ________________________________

The Day's Tasks

P0 Tasks :

⊙ ________________________________ ☐

⊙ ________________________________ ☐

P1 Task : ________________________________ ☐

P2 Task : ________________________________ ☐

Daily Gratitude

★ I'm grateful for ________________________________

★ I'm grateful for ________________________________

★ I'm grateful for ________________________________

Date:__/__/____

My Priorities

Priority 0 (P0):

Priority 1 (P1) :

Priority 2 (P2):

The Day's Tasks

P0 Tasks :

☐

☐

P1 Task :   ☐

P2 Task :   ☐

Daily Gratitude

✴ I'm grateful for

✴ I'm grateful for

✴ I'm grateful for

Date:__/__/____

My Priorities

Priority 0 (P0): ______________________________

Priority 1 (P1) : ______________________________

Priority 2 (P2): ______________________________

The Day's Tasks

P0 Tasks :

☐

☐

P1 Task : ☐

P2 Task : ☐

🪷 Daily Gratitude

⭐ I'm grateful for ______________________________

⭐ I'm grateful for ______________________________

⭐ I'm grateful for ______________________________

Date:__ / __ / ____

My Priorities

Priority 0 (P0): ____

Priority 1 (P1) : ____

Priority 2 (P2): ____

The Day's Tasks

P0 Tasks :

☐

☐

P1 Task : ☐

P2 Task : ☐

✿ Daily Gratitude

✳ I'm grateful for ____

✳ I'm grateful for ____

✳ I'm grateful for ____

Date:__/__/____

My Priorities

Priority 0 (P0): _______________________________

Priority 1 (P1) : _______________________________

Priority 2 (P2): _______________________________

The Day's Tasks

P0 Tasks :

- ☐

- ☐

P1 Task : ☐

P2 Task : ☐

Daily Gratitude

⋆ I'm grateful for _______________________________

⋆ I'm grateful for _______________________________

⋆ I'm grateful for _______________________________

Date:__/__/____

My Priorities

Priority 0 (P0):

Priority 1 (P1) :

Priority 2 (P2):

The Day's Tasks

P0 Tasks :

☐

☐

P1 Task : ☐

P2 Task : ☐

Daily Gratitude

⭐ I'm grateful for

⭐ I'm grateful for

⭐ I'm grateful for

Date:__ / __ / ____

My Priorities

Priority 0 (P0): ____

Priority 1 (P1) : ____

Priority 2 (P2): ____

The Day's Tasks

P0 Tasks :

- ☐

- ☐

P1 Task : ☐

P2 Task : ☐

Daily Gratitude

⋆ I'm grateful for _______________________________________

⋆ I'm grateful for _______________________________________

⋆ I'm grateful for _______________________________________

Date:__/__/____

My Priorities

Priority 0 (P0): _______________________________________

Priority 1 (P1) : _______________________________________

Priority 2 (P2): _______________________________________

The Day's Tasks

P0 Tasks :

⬚

⬚

P1 Task : ⬚

P2 Task : ⬚

🪷 Daily Gratitude

✦ I'm grateful for _______________________________________

✦ I'm grateful for _______________________________________

✦ I'm grateful for _______________________________________

Date:__/__/____

My Priorities

Priority 0 (P0): ___________________________________

Priority 1 (P1) : ___________________________________

Priority 2 (P2): ___________________________________

The Day's Tasks

P0 Tasks :

☐

☐

P1 Task : ☐

P2 Task : ☐

🪷 Daily Gratitude

★ I'm grateful for ___________________________________

★ I'm grateful for ___________________________________

★ I'm grateful for ___________________________________

Date:__/__/____

My Priorities

Priority 0 (P0): ________________________________

Priority 1 (P1) : ________________________________

Priority 2 (P2): ________________________________

The Day's Tasks

P0 Tasks :

☐

☐

P1 Task : ☐

P2 Task : ☐

Daily Gratitude

☀ I'm grateful for ________________________________

☀ I'm grateful for ________________________________

☀ I'm grateful for ________________________________

Date:__/__/____

My Priorities

Priority 0 (P0): _______________________________

Priority 1 (P1) : _______________________________

Priority 2 (P2): _______________________________

The Day's Tasks

P0 Tasks :

⬜

⬜

P1 Task : ⬜

P2 Task : ⬜

🪷 Daily Gratitude

⭐ I'm grateful for _______________________________

⭐ I'm grateful for _______________________________

⭐ I'm grateful for _______________________________

Date:__/__/____

My Priorities

Priority 0 (P0):

Priority 1 (P1) :

Priority 2 (P2):

The Day's Tasks

P0 Tasks :

☐

☐

P1 Task : ☐

P2 Task : ☐

🪷 Daily Gratitude

⭐ I'm grateful for

⭐ I'm grateful for

⭐ I'm grateful for

Date:__/__/____

My Priorities

Priority 0 (P0): ________________________

Priority 1 (P1) : ________________________

Priority 2 (P2): ________________________

The Day's Tasks

P0 Tasks :

- ________________________ ☐

- ________________________ ☐

P1 Task : ________________________ ☐

P2 Task : ________________________ ☐

Daily Gratitude

★ I'm grateful for ________________________

★ I'm grateful for ________________________

★ I'm grateful for ________________________

Date:__/__/____

My Priorities

Priority 0 (P0): ____

Priority 1 (P1) : ____

Priority 2 (P2): ____

The Day's Tasks

P0 Tasks :

☐

☐

P1 Task : ☐

P2 Task : ☐

Daily Gratitude

⭐ I'm grateful for ____

⭐ I'm grateful for ____

⭐ I'm grateful for ____

Date:__/__/____

My Priorities

Priority 0 (P0): ____

Priority 1 (P1) : ____

Priority 2 (P2): ____

The Day's Tasks

P0 Tasks :

⬡ ☐
____

⬡ ☐
____

P1 Task : ☐

P2 Task : ☐

🪷 Daily Gratitude

★ I'm grateful for _______________________________________

★ I'm grateful for _______________________________________

★ I'm grateful for _______________________________________

Date:__/__/____

My Priorities

Priority 0 (P0):

Priority 1 (P1) :

Priority 2 (P2):

The Day's Tasks

P0 Tasks :

☐

☐

P1 Task : ☐

P2 Task : ☐

Daily Gratitude

☆ I'm grateful for

☆ I'm grateful for

☆ I'm grateful for

Date:___/___/_____

My Priorities

Priority 0 (P0):

Priority 1 (P1) :

Priority 2 (P2):

The Day's Tasks

P0 Tasks :

☐

☐

P1 Task : ☐

P2 Task : ☐

Daily Gratitude

⭐ I'm grateful for

⭐ I'm grateful for

⭐ I'm grateful for

Date:__/__/____

My Priorities

Priority 0 (P0):

Priority 1 (P1) :

Priority 2 (P2):

The Day's Tasks

P0 Tasks :

☐

☐

P1 Task : ☐

P2 Task : ☐

 **Daily Gratitude**

⭐ I'm grateful for

⭐ I'm grateful for

⭐ I'm grateful for

Date:__/__/____

My Priorities

Priority 0 (P0):

Priority 1 (P1) :

Priority 2 (P2):

The Day's Tasks

P0 Tasks :

☐

☐

P1 Task : ☐

P2 Task : ☐

Daily Gratitude

⁎ I'm grateful for

⁎ I'm grateful for

⁎ I'm grateful for

Date:__/__/____

My Priorities

Priority 0 (P0): _______________________________

Priority 1 (P1) : _______________________________

Priority 2 (P2): _______________________________

The Day's Tasks

P0 Tasks :

☐

☐

P1 Task : ☐

P2 Task : ☐

Daily Gratitude

⭐ I'm grateful for _______________________________

⭐ I'm grateful for _______________________________

⭐ I'm grateful for _______________________________

Date:__/__/____

My Priorities

Priority 0 (P0): _______________________________

Priority 1 (P1) : _______________________________

Priority 2 (P2): _______________________________

The Day's Tasks

P0 Tasks :

- ☐

- ☐

P1 Task : ☐

P2 Task : ☐

🪷 Daily Gratitude

⭐ I'm grateful for _______________________________

⭐ I'm grateful for _______________________________

⭐ I'm grateful for _______________________________

Date:__/__/____

My Priorities

Priority 0 (P0): _______________________________________

Priority 1 (P1) : _______________________________________

Priority 2 (P2): _______________________________________

The Day's Tasks

PO Tasks :

☐

☐

P1 Task : ☐

P2 Task : ☐

Daily Gratitude

✶ I'm grateful for _______________________________________

✶ I'm grateful for _______________________________________

✶ I'm grateful for _______________________________________

Date:__/__/____

My Priorities

Priority 0 (P0): ___________________________________

Priority 1 (P1) : __________________________________

Priority 2 (P2): ___________________________________

The Day's Tasks

P0 Tasks :

- ____________________________________ ☐

- ____________________________________ ☐

P1 Task : __________________________ ☐

P2 Task : ___________________________ ☐

❀ Daily Gratitude

★ I'm grateful for ________________________________

★ I'm grateful for ________________________________

★ I'm grateful for ________________________________

Date:__/__/____

My Priorities

Priority 0 (P0): _______________________________

Priority 1 (P1) : _______________________________

Priority 2 (P2): _______________________________

The Day's Tasks

P0 Tasks :

☐

☐

P1 Task : ☐

P2 Task : ☐

Daily Gratitude

☆ I'm grateful for _______________________________

☆ I'm grateful for _______________________________

☆ I'm grateful for _______________________________

Date:__/__/____

My Priorities

Priority 0 (P0): _______________________________

Priority 1 (P1) : _______________________________

Priority 2 (P2): _______________________________

The Day's Tasks

P0 Tasks :

☐

☐

P1 Task :　☐

P2 Task :　☐

✿ Daily Gratitude

✷ I'm grateful for _______________________________

✷ I'm grateful for _______________________________

✷ I'm grateful for _______________________________

Date:__/__/____

My Priorities

Priority 0 (P0): _______________________________________

Priority 1 (P1) : _______________________________________

Priority 2 (P2): _______________________________________

The Day's Tasks

P0 Tasks :

☐

☐

P1 Task : ☐

P2 Task : ☐

Daily Gratitude

✸ I'm grateful for _______________________________________

✸ I'm grateful for _______________________________________

✸ I'm grateful for _______________________________________

Date:__ / __ / ____

My Priorities

Priority 0 (P0): _______________________________________

Priority 1 (P1) : _______________________________________

Priority 2 (P2): _______________________________________

The Day's Tasks

P0 Tasks :

☐

☐

P1 Task : ☐

P2 Task : ☐

❀ Daily Gratitude

★ I'm grateful for _______________________________________

★ I'm grateful for _______________________________________

★ I'm grateful for _______________________________________

Date:__/__/____

My Priorities

Priority 0 (P0): ___________________________

Priority 1 (P1) : ___________________________

Priority 2 (P2): ___________________________

The Day's Tasks

P0 Tasks :

☐

☐

P1 Task : ☐

P2 Task : ☐

🪷 Daily Gratitude

✳ I'm grateful for ___________________________

✳ I'm grateful for ___________________________

✳ I'm grateful for ___________________________

Date:__/__/____

My Priorities

Priority 0 (P0): _______________________________________

Priority 1 (P1) : _______________________________________

Priority 2 (P2): _______________________________________

The Day's Tasks

P0 Tasks :

⚬ _______________________________________ ☐

⚬ _______________________________________ ☐

P1 Task : _______________________________ ☐

P2 Task : ________________________________ ☐

✿ Daily Gratitude

✦ I'm grateful for _______________________________________

✦ I'm grateful for _______________________________________

✦ I'm grateful for _______________________________________

Date:__/__/____

My Priorities

Priority 0 (P0): _______________________

Priority 1 (P1) : _______________________

Priority 2 (P2): _______________________

The Day's Tasks

P0 Tasks :

☐

☐

P1 Task : ☐

P2 Task : ☐

Daily Gratitude

★ I'm grateful for _______________________

★ I'm grateful for _______________________

★ I'm grateful for _______________________

Date:__/__/____

My Priorities

Priority 0 (P0): _______________________________

Priority 1 (P1) : _______________________________

Priority 2 (P2): _______________________________

The Day's Tasks

P0 Tasks :

☐

☐

P1 Task : ☐

P2 Task : ☐

Daily Gratitude

★ I'm grateful for _______________________________

★ I'm grateful for _______________________________

★ I'm grateful for _______________________________

Date:__/__/____

My Priorities

Priority 0 (P0): ________________________

Priority 1 (P1) : ________________________

Priority 2 (P2): ________________________

The Day's Tasks

P0 Tasks :

☐ ________________________

☐ ________________________

P1 Task : ☐ ________________________

P2 Task : ☐ ________________________

Daily Gratitude

☆ I'm grateful for ________________________

☆ I'm grateful for ________________________

☆ I'm grateful for ________________________

Date:__/__/____

My Priorities

Priority 0 (P0):

Priority 1 (P1) :

Priority 2 (P2):

The Day's Tasks

P0 Tasks :

☐

☐

P1 Task : ☐

P2 Task : ☐

❀ Daily Gratitude

★ I'm grateful for

★ I'm grateful for

★ I'm grateful for

Date:__/__/____

My Priorities

Priority 0 (P0): ____

Priority 1 (P1) : ____

Priority 2 (P2): ____

The Day's Tasks

P0 Tasks :

☐

☐

P1 Task : ☐

P2 Task : ☐

🪷 Daily Gratitude

✶ I'm grateful for ____

✶ I'm grateful for ____

✶ I'm grateful for ____

Date:__/__/____

My Priorities

Priority 0 (P0):

Priority 1 (P1) :

Priority 2 (P2):

The Day's Tasks

P0 Tasks :

P1 Task :

P2 Task :

Daily Gratitude

⭐ I'm grateful for

⭐ I'm grateful for

⭐ I'm grateful for

Date:__/__/____

My Priorities

Priority 0 (P0): ________________________________

Priority 1 (P1) : ________________________________

Priority 2 (P2): ________________________________

The Day's Tasks

P0 Tasks :

☐

☐

P1 Task : ☐

P2 Task : ☐

Daily Gratitude

☆ I'm grateful for ________________________________

☆ I'm grateful for ________________________________

☆ I'm grateful for ________________________________

Date:__/__/____

My Priorities

Priority 0 (P0): ________________________________

Priority 1 (P1) : ________________________________

Priority 2 (P2): ________________________________

The Day's Tasks

P0 Tasks :

⊙ ________________________________ ☐

⊙ ________________________________ ☐

P1 Task : ________________________________ ☐

P2 Task : ________________________________ ☐

🪷 Daily Gratitude

✦ I'm grateful for ________________________________

✦ I'm grateful for ________________________________

✦ I'm grateful for ________________________________

# Last 9 Days Left...

By now, bullet journaling must be an interminable part of your life...

But there are only 9 journal pages left!

Order a New Copy Now - so, it arrives before *this* Journal runs out.

The *easiest* way to keep a developed habit alive is to "*Avoid Breaking The Chain*"

Keep your journaling habit chain going

Just scan the QR code below to order a new journal fresh off the press!

Date:__/__/____

My Priorities

Priority 0 (P0): ____

Priority 1 (P1) : ____

Priority 2 (P2): ____

The Day's Tasks

P0 Tasks :

- ☐

- ☐

P1 Task : ☐

P2 Task : ☐

🪷 Daily Gratitude

⭐ I'm grateful for ____

⭐ I'm grateful for ____

⭐ I'm grateful for ____

Date:__/__/____

My Priorities

Priority 0 (P0): ____

Priority 1 (P1) : ____

Priority 2 (P2): ____

The Day's Tasks

P0 Tasks :

☐

☐

P1 Task : ☐

P2 Task : ☐

Daily Gratitude

✳ I'm grateful for ____

✳ I'm grateful for ____

✳ I'm grateful for ____

Date:__/__/____

My Priorities

Priority 0 (P0): ____

Priority 1 (P1) : ____

Priority 2 (P2): ____

The Day's Tasks

P0 Tasks :

- ☐

- ☐

P1 Task : ☐

P2 Task : ☐

🪷 Daily Gratitude

⭐ I'm grateful for ____

⭐ I'm grateful for ____

⭐ I'm grateful for ____

Date:__/__/____

My Priorities

Priority 0 (P0): ________________________________

Priority 1 (P1) : ________________________________

Priority 2 (P2): ________________________________

The Day's Tasks

P0 Tasks :

☐ ________________________________

☐ ________________________________

P1 Task : ☐ ________________________________

P2 Task : ☐ ________________________________

Daily Gratitude

* I'm grateful for ________________________________

* I'm grateful for ________________________________

* I'm grateful for ________________________________

Date:__/__/____

My Priorities

Priority 0 (P0):

Priority 1 (P1) :

Priority 2 (P2):

The Day's Tasks

P0 Tasks :

☐

☐

P1 Task : ☐

P2 Task : ☐

🪷 Daily Gratitude

⭐ I'm grateful for

⭐ I'm grateful for

⭐ I'm grateful for

Date:__/__/____

My Priorities

Priority 0 (P0): ___________________________

Priority 1 (P1) : ___________________________

Priority 2 (P2): ___________________________

The Day's Tasks

P0 Tasks :

* ___________________________ ☐

* ___________________________ ☐

P1 Task : ___________________________ ☐

P2 Task : ___________________________ ☐

Daily Gratitude

* I'm grateful for ___________________________

* I'm grateful for ___________________________

* I'm grateful for ___________________________

Date:__/__/____

My Priorities

Priority 0 (P0): ________________________________

Priority 1 (P1) : ________________________________

Priority 2 (P2): ________________________________

The Day's Tasks

P0 Tasks :

- ☐

- ☐

P1 Task : ☐

P2 Task : ☐

✿ Daily Gratitude

★ I'm grateful for ________________________________

★ I'm grateful for ________________________________

★ I'm grateful for ________________________________

Date:__/__/____

My Priorities

Priority 0 (P0):

Priority 1 (P1) :

Priority 2 (P2):

The Day's Tasks

P0 Tasks :

☐

☐

P1 Task : ☐

P2 Task : ☐

Daily Gratitude

✳ I'm grateful for

✳ I'm grateful for

✳ I'm grateful for

Date:__/__/____

My Priorities

Priority 0 (P0): ____

Priority 1 (P1) : ____

Priority 2 (P2): ____

The Day's Tasks

P0 Tasks :

- ____ ☐

- ____ ☐

P1 Task : ____ ☐

P2 Task : ____ ☐

Daily Gratitude

✶ I'm grateful for ____

✶ I'm grateful for ____

✶ I'm grateful for ____

3 Months In...

This Journal is a quarterly album of your tasks, priorities, and expressions of gratitude.

Don't dump it in the bin. Instead, preserve it...

Somewhere safe so when you chance upon it years later, you can reflect.

This Journal bids you Goodbye! Hope your New copy has arrived by now.

See you there

Found This Journal Useful? 

I'd greatly appreciate an **Amazon Rating** and **Review** if you liked this journal.

To save you time, the QR code on the right will take you directly to the review page.

Thank you for helping this journal reach other deserving hands.

@neeramitra

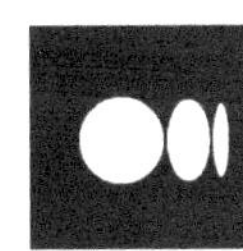

medium.com/ @neeramitra-reddy

@neeramitra reddy1207